I Do He Didn't

Gina Lee

Published by Gina Lee, 2023.

While every precaution has been taken in the preparation of this book, the publisher assumes no responsibility for errors or omissions, or for damages resulting from the use of the information contained herein.

I DO HE DIDN'T

I do He didn't

By Gina Lee

Copyright © 2023 by Gina Lee

Published by Gina Lee

Scriptures marked NIV are taken from the HOLY BIBLE New International Version Copyright 1973, 1978, 1984 by International Bible Society. Used by permission of Zondervan Publishing House.

Some paragraphs with quotation marks around definitions of Narcissist, Trauma Bonding, Love Bonding, Gaslighting, Serial Cheater, and Emotional and Verbal Abuse. Are taken from the following websites:

Everyday Health www.everydayhealth.com,

www.webmd.com,

www.banyanmentalhealth.com,

www.psychcentral.com,

www.quora.com,

www.athensreview.com,

www.calendar-australia.com,

www.healthline.com,

www.joannalipari.medium.com,

National Domestic Violence Hotline wwwthehotline.org.

The author of this book does not dispense medical, legal, or psychological advice or prescribe the use of any technique as a form of treatment for physical, emotional, or medical problems without the advice of a physician. The intent of the author is only to offer information of a general nature to help you in your quest for emotional and spiritual well-being. In the event you use any of the information in this book, the author does not assume responsibility for your actions.

No part of this book may be reproduced, stored in a retrieval system, or transmitted by any means, electronic, mechanical, photocopying, recording, or otherwise, without written permission from the author. All rights reserved. Printed in the USA.

Cover design by: Dayne McNutt and Getcovers

The views and content expressed in this book are those of the author.

By reading this document, the reader agrees that under no circumstances is the author responsible for any losses, direct or indirect, that are incurred as a result of the use of the information contained within the document, including, but not limited to errors, omissions, or inaccuracies.

I have changed all names and places to protect the privacy of individuals.

Acknowledgment

I am grateful for my parents and their unwavering support. Especially when they were unaware of my struggles and I needed them the most. I thank them for being there to support me when I could not support myself. The unconditional love they have shown me is something that I will always be grateful for.

I owe a debt of gratitude to all my friends and family who stood by me, picked me up, and helped put me back together when I was broken. I will always be thankful for them.

The person to whom I owe a great deal of gratitude is my pastor Jeff, who has served as my shepherd and counselor. Showing me God never left or gave up on me.

A trio of ladies who listened to me aided my journey toward healing, prayed with me, and taught me how to forgive. It is my deepest desire and prayer that God will equip me to be a beacon of hope and encouragement to anyone else who is going through their own struggles and dark days.

My real-life angel Earl. Thank you for your devotion to follow God's will. Your willingness to obey what God wanted you to do, by getting involved in a stranger's life. You helped save me by letting me see the truth about my marriage.

I am forever thankful to my dear friends Connie, Tracy, & Sherrie who generously offered their time and skills to read and help edit this story.

Dedication

This dedication expresses my love and admiration for my 3 sons and acknowledges the significant role they have played in my life. Despite the darkness and loneliness I experienced, they served as my bright star to get through it all.

CONTENTS

INTRODUCTION

My name is Gina. I am from a small town in the heart of America. I grew up in a normal family. My dad owned his own business, and we went to church on Sundays. I have two older brothers and two younger brothers, which makes me the princess in the middle. We ate dinner together and worked hard together as a family. My family taught me that God loves me, and he sent his son Jesus to die on the cross to be raised again in 3 days for my sins. At 12, I asked Jesus into my heart, and I was baptized.

For God so loved the world that he gave his one and only Son, that whoever believes in him shall not perish but have eternal life. John 3:16 (NIV)

I was just like every normal little girl. I played with Barbies, played house, and fought with my brothers. My parents shielded me from the world outside and kept me innocent.

Like all the little girls, I dreamed about my wedding. I put a towel on my head to pretend like it was my veil. I collected dandelions for my bouquet and marched down the sidewalk as if it were the aisle of the church. As I grew, a little older, my dreams changed a little. I got more imaginative about what I wanted my colors to be, the cake that I wanted to eat, and the music that I wanted to play. As a teenager, my dreams evolved. I dreamed of Prince Charming waiting for me at the end of the aisle. He was tall, dark, and handsome. I used to dream of being treated like a princess by him, hearing wonderful things, receiving gifts, and living happily ever after. I dreamed about the home we would live in, with the playground in the backyard. How many children would we have? What vacations will we take as a family? All I needed to do was find my Prince Charming. At the ripe old age of 20, I thought I had found him. So, I said I do, but little did I know he didn't.

T*his is my story. A story of dreams, hope, love, betrayal, abuse, adultery, healing, forgiveness, and a new hope.*

Chapter 1

Young love meeting for the first time

God brings people into our lives for a moment, a season, or a lifetime. We might not always understand the reason someone was brought into our lives. We just need to have faith that God has a plan for us.

After High School, I did not know what I wanted to do with my life. I started a new job at a local clothing store. I loved that job. Mr. Locke gave me a lot of responsibility. One, I made the store deposit at the bank every day at the same time. Down the block and across the street, I would walk. I was unaware that I was being observed daily by a tall, dark, and handsome man from the 4th floor of the bank building. One afternoon after making the deposit, I came out of the bank; I went to the light to cross the street and there stood this tall, handsome man with dark hair and eyes to match. There was a polite exchange of greetings between us. Then I kept walking back to work.

A few days later, this same handsome guy came into the store. Now Mr. Locke was old-fashioned. He would not allow me to wait on the men, so Mr. Locke helped him. This mystery man walked around the store looking at everything but looking at nothing. I would stand over in the women's dresses staring at him. In the following weeks, he continued to come in more and more often. By this time, I am sure he had enough socks and underwear to last a lifetime. Sometimes he would bring in a friend. After some interaction with them, I could gather that the names of the two individuals were Tom and Paul. Over several weeks, I engaged in conversation with them regularly. As time passed, I started to feel like a genuine friendship was developing.

One Monday afternoon when Tom and Paul were leaving the store. Paul said to me,

"I am having a Hawaiian luau at my house this weekend. Would you be willing to accompany Tom to it?"

I accepted the invitation. I exchanged phone numbers with Tom. That was the beginning of hours of nightly phone calls. The next four months were a blur. Tom swept me away with all the romance.

Being inexperienced with dating, I was unaware of all the red flags I was missing. Such as the simple inability to tell the truth. I eventually came to the conclusion he was not being truthful about almost everything. He lied about things that would not matter to anybody, especially me. I did not care about the vehicles he said he owned. Claiming that they were being stored in garages in another state. I later realized he wasn't truthful about the jobs that he had. He told me things like he could have gone to the Olympics for swimming. He even convinced me that the military wanted him for the Special Forces, but he couldn't go because he had to stay home to take care of his younger brother. He found it necessary to lie about it all.

Save me, Lord, from lying lips and from deceitful tongues. Psalm 120:2 (NIV)

(In my healing, I have learned. When the narcissist lies, he or she is trying to make themselves appear dominant. They lie for self-gain, believing that telling mistruths makes them look smarter than the other person. Having a victim at their side to whom they can lie provides them with a constant narcissistic supply, someone that fuels their sickness.) Everyday Health www.everydayhealth.com

The first impression I had of this guy was that he was an exceptional individual. To maintain our relationship, I felt it was important to be truthful with him. I wanted to share the reality of who I am with him and let him understand everything. This seems to be the right thing to do when you love someone. No one ever discovered the secret I had held. Hiding it has become second nature to me and I've learned to live with it. Feeling extremely vulnerable about it. I decided he should know. Taking a moment and a deep breath. I began,

"I need to tell you something about myself. I have dyslexia. They determined my diagnosis when I was in the first grade."

Dyslexia is a learning disorder that involves difficulty reading because of problems identifying speech sounds and learning how they relate to letters and words.

"Reading is a challenge for me and I'm not great at spelling." I sat there, waiting for him to respond. I am not sure what I wanted him to say. Maybe more than what I got. He casually said,

"OKAY, you need to practice some more."

At that moment, I did not understand that I had just transferred power into his hands, and the hardship it would cause me in the future.

Love is patient, love is kind. It does not envy; it does not boast; it is not proud. It is not rude; it is not self-seeking; it is not easily angered; it keeps no record of wrongs. Love does not delight in evil but rejoices with the truth. It always protects, always trusts, always hopes, always perseveres. 1 Corinthians 13:4-7 (NIV)

What I didn't understand at the time was lack of empathy is another sign of narcissism. (This means that the narcissist is unwilling or unable to empathize with the needs, wants, or feelings of other people.)wedmd.com This also makes it difficult for them to take responsibility for their behavior. Narcissism is a personality disorder that affects a considerable portion of the world's population, including both men and women. Narcissists have an exaggerated sense of self-importance and feelings of entitlement, coupled with a lack of empathy toward others. The behaviors of a narcissist can have serious consequences on those around them, particularly in intimate relationships.

Chapter 2

Proposal to the wedding vows

Sometimes love can happen quickly. There are times when lust can be mistaken for love. And we need to be careful not to confuse the two, or we might find ourselves in situations we can't get out of. One powerful realization is that everything happens for a reason, because it's preparing you for what's coming in life.

Tom was very smooth and swift to sweep me off my feet. We talked about marriage in the first few weeks of dating. In four short months, while sitting on his couch, he pulled a ring out of his pocket and asked.

"Will you marry me?"

There was no trace of romance. I am not entirely sure if he went down on one knee to ask for my hand in marriage.

This was not what I had dreamed it would be. I was excited nonetheless that someone loved me so much that they wanted to marry me.

He who finds a wife finds what is good and receives favor from the Lord. Proverbs 18:22 (NIV)

Tom wanted to get married right away. He chose the date April 23rd, 1988, which gave me four months to plan the wedding. So, my grandma, mom, and I went to work quickly, planning a wedding. But it was far from easy. Tom had an opinion about everything! He did not like most of my ideas and insisted things go his way. However, he did not have a penny to contribute to our wedding. I was fortunate enough to be in a family where we did not need to worry about expenses. I did not care that he lacked the money. What I did care about was not being able to have my dream wedding. The wedding I had dreamed about my whole life. I did desire to please him, so I gave in on a lot of things.

Better to live on a corner of the roof than share a house with a quarrelsome wife. Proverbs 21:9 (NIV)

Tom was capable of being romantic when he wanted to be, and he had the perfect phrases to make me feel appreciated. He would go by the local florist shop to buy a single red rose. And bring it to me at work. He would do this several days in a row. That made me feel so loved. During the evenings, he would spend hours chatting with me on the phone. He had a gift for making me feel special with the words he spoke. I believed Tom was so smart and right about everything. I wanted to ensure he was always happy.

A narcissist in a romantic relationship is likely to engage in a technique called love bombing. Love bombing is a manipulative strategy that uses grand romantic gestures, excessive praise, and extreme flattery that is aimed at overwhelming their partner with love and affection. This strategy aims to create an illusion of a perfect and all-consuming relationship which the new partner cannot do without them. This strategy can be effective because the

*new partner has not yet had the opportunity to get to know them
well, and their behavior may appear endearing and genuine.*

The four months seemed to pass by in the blink of an eye, but
thankfully, with the amazing support of my family, we were able
to plan the wedding. Some of my family did not want me to get
married to Tom. They felt something off about him, especially
my dad. Tom made a few relatives of mine very uncomfortable
when he was around them. I didn't understand why. He just gave
off a particular vibe, they would tell me.

On the day of our wedding before my dad and I walked down
the aisle. My dad turned to me and said.

"If you do not want to do this, we can leave right now."

But the doors opened, and down the aisle, we walked.

**For this reason, a man will leave his father and mother and
be united to his wife, and they will become one flesh. Genesis
2:24 (NIV)**

Tom also wished to take control of the honeymoon. He wanted
to make all the plans. He determined Branson was the
destination for a few days. From my perspective, it was
remarkable. We came home to a little house that we had rented
before the wedding. I would like to say that it was marital bliss
from day one.

But right away, I encountered the challenge of not knowing how
to do things the way he wanted them done. I'll never forget to
this day our first fight. The fight was over how I put the bread
away. He gave me a 30-minute lesson on how to press the air out

of the bag. Twist up the bag tight, put the tie around, and twist it three times. Take the extra part of the bag and fold it down over the loaf and set it flat on the counter. I can find the humor in it now, but at the time it was not funny. This was the start of my lessons on how to do things right.

I got lessons on how to fold his socks, underwear and how to put them away in the drawer. He instructed me on how to iron, wash dishes, drive, and even cook.

Having dyslexia is hard and embarrassing. Tom made me feel like I was completely putting him out if I asked him to spell words for me. I would explain that I wasn't doing it just to make him mad at me, but it didn't matter. He would just make me feel stupid.

As the saying goes, "A cord of three strands is not easily broken." In a marriage, those three strands should be the husband, wife, and God. It is crucial to remember that putting God at the center of your relationship strengthens the bond between you and your spouse. Without God as the firm foundation, a marriage can quickly fall apart.

Through the triangle of husband, wife, and God, we learn that communication, respect, and commitment are critical in a successful marriage. As we grow closer to God individually, we grow closer to each other as well. We learn to love and forgive more readily, to be selfless and understanding, and to put the needs of our spouse above our own. By seeking God's guidance and wisdom in our marriage. We gain the ability to navigate through challenges, support each other through the good and bad, and find joy and fulfillment in each other's company. Thus, putting God at the center of one's marriage is essential to not only a healthy relationship but also a lifetime of love, trust, and happiness.

One thing I looked forward to was being able to pray with my husband. I was always told spouses that pray together would grow stronger in their marriage and grow closer to God. That was something I wanted. The first night I asked him to pray together, Tom said,

"You go first."

We were lying in bed holding hands. I started talking to God, just as I always had. His soft laughter caught my attention. I stopped and asked,

"Is there something wrong?"

He exclaimed, "Is that how you pray?"

It mortified me. Nobody had told me that there was a correct method of prayer. He informed me that there was a right way to pray, and I was doing it wrong. That night broke my heart. I was ashamed that I did not even know how to pray. He told me this is how you pray. Tom began to pray as if he were in front of the church. He was using a lot of big words and he just went on and on. To tell you the truth, I am not sure even what he was praying about. From that night on, I never prayed aloud again.

And when you pray, do not keep on babbling like pagans, for they think they will be heard because of their many words. Matthew 6:7 (NIV)

Tom and I had a lot of fun together, engaging in various activities and spending quality time together. To say that Tom could always make me laugh is an understatement. He had an uncanny ability to bring humor to any situation. We both loved playing softball. We could spend hours in the evening in the backyard, throwing the ball back and forth with each other. Something so simple, but we enjoyed every minute. We got in the habit of playing the card game War every night before we went to sleep. As far as I believed, we were both Christians, and we always went to church together. That was significant to me. I was so lucky that he wanted me. During these moments, I was so happy that I was married to Tom. I hoped we would have a wonderful life together. I thought I just needed to change a few things to improve myself, to become a better wife for him. Changing a few things didn't seem like a difficult task to me.

A friend gave me a book on the 5 Love Languages. The book had become popular, and she thought I would like it. I was eager to learn what we both needed from each other. I discovered my love language is physical touch and words of affirmation. However, Tom hated to be touched. He would move away from me every time I tried to even touch his arm. Sometimes he would make a big scene by huffing and throwing his arm away from me.

I would always try to look my best every time we went out, but he never seemed to notice. His giving me the words of affirmation I needed rarely happened. He rarely even told me he loved me. What was his love language? I do not know. I tested all 5 love languages, but nothing seemed to make him happy.

The next five years seem to go by quickly. Mostly, we got along well. It was peculiar that he treated me kindly during certain weeks. We could talk about anything. We would spend the evening playing games or going for walks, just enjoying being with each other. But then, just as the tides turn, sometimes he could be downright rude and mean to me. A pattern was forming, and I could see it. I just did not know what it meant.

In the early 1990s, we moved to the Northern part of Oklahoma. We found a magnificent church to be a part of, and we joined the young married class. I loved being with all of them. Some of my best friends to this day came from that group. We were all together every weekend. But something was not right with Tom. While the group was together, Tom would do things like put his arm around my head and give me a Nuggie. It was embarrassing. He would also say hurtful things to me, just trying to be funny. I could tell Tom was making everyone uncomfortable with the way he would treat and talked to me. I just pretended to be ok, even though I was dying inside.

I always knew Tom could be a huge flirt; He would always chat it up with the waitresses, acting like I was not even at the table. He always made me feel small and unseen in those moments.

I remember one date night we went Putt Putting. The young girl behind the counter, Tom thought, was beautiful. He flirted with her the entire evening. When I got upset about it, he said I was being overly emotional and that he was just being polite. This kind of behavior happened a lot when we were out together.

Cheating is a term used to describe the act of being unfaithful in a relationship. What makes up cheating can vary from person to person and relationship to relationship, but some common examples may include:

*1. **Sexual infidelity**: Having sexual contact with someone outside of the committed relationship.*

*2. **Emotional infidelity**: Developing an emotional attachment or romantic relationship with someone outside of the committed relationship.*

*3. **Cyber infidelity**: Utilizing social media or other digital means to engage in romantic or sexual conversations with someone outside the committed relationship.*

*4. **Non-physical deception**: Participating in activities or interactions that are kept hidden from the partner.*

Ultimately, cheating is any behavior that violates the trust and intimacy of a romantic partner. Which can include sexting, being secretly active on a dating site, lap dances, kissing, flirting, and breaking rules or boundaries established within the relationship.

Have you ever felt like your head was going to explode, but you knew you must hold it together? This is how I felt most of the time, like I was losing my mind. Tom continued over the years to be very subtle in the ways he corrected me. He corrected the way I spoke and told stories. He would interrupt by saying,

"No, actually, it was this way or that way."

The word ACTUALLY is a word I have grown to hate. He corrected the way I did almost everything. I taught myself to shut down and retreat in myself. This way, his words didn't hurt so badly.

Husbands, in the same way, be considerate as you live with your wives, and treat them with respect as the weaker partner and as heirs with you of the gracious gift of life, so that nothing will hinder your prayers. 1 Peter 3:7 (NIV)

I started praying to God, asking him to please show me the things that Tom was trying to hide from me. And please give me the discernment to know the truth. Something started happening to me. There was a voice in my head. There was no audible voice. I didn't see flashes of light or flying objects. There was no writing in the mirror. But I knew what this voice was telling me.

Whether you turn to the right or to the left, your ears will hear a voice behind you, saying, "This is the way; walk in it." Isaiah 30:21 (NIV)

I believe God gives us warning signs. It is up to us to follow them.

Chapter 3

The first few years of deceit

Pay attention to your gut feeling. No matter how lovely something looks, if it doesn't feel right, it probably isn't. God uses both careful deliberation and intuition to guide us. This gut instinct of the Spirit is often God's way of helping you to have caution concerning other people.

In 1992, we were expecting our first son. Eager like all new moms would be. I had a beautiful, healthy, perfect son. We were home from the hospital for the first couple of days when the phone rang. The lady on the other end asked for my husband by name. I gave the phone to Tom. He talked a bit and then hung up. When I asked him who that lady was, he told me the girl's name. It was his ex-fiancée. He explained she was calling to congratulate him on having a son. However, I did not understand why she would call him. Of course, he dismissed me, saying it was only her calling to congratulate us. Tom told me I needed to stop, and I had nothing to worry about. Now let me remind you that in 1992, we did not have cell phones. We did not have the internet. I didn't have a computer with Facebook to let the entire world know that I had a baby. If people knew things, you had to tell them personally. How and why would his ex-fiancé even know about us? With my young mom's brain not comprehending how she could have known that we were having a baby or even home from the hospital, I let it go.

Fast forward three years later to 1995. I was seven months pregnant with our 2nd son. Tom worked a lot of hours and a lot of overtime. He even had some meetings out of town on the weekends. I never complained about it. I knew he was doing it all for his family.

Early in our marriage, Tom had introduced me to some of his long-life friends, Collin, and Nancy. Nancy and I became close over the years. Nancy called one afternoon out of the blue. We chatted for a while, then she asked if Tom was going to be home this weekend. I said,

"No, he has meetings out of town for a few days."

Nancy began to speak, "Gina, I need to tell you something. I don't wish to hurt you, but I feel like I ought to let you know something I have found out. Tom has been talking to his ex-fiancé. He is planning on meeting with her this weekend at a hotel."

I felt as though someone had punched me in my gut. I could not breathe. The entire world stopped for a minute. How could this be happening to me? As I sat there with the phone in my hand sobbing, I told my friend I would need to give her a callback. I hung up and called Tom at work and told him he needed to get home immediately. When he got home, I confronted him and told him what I knew. He admitted he had been talking to her, but they were just friends. They had made plans to meet and catch up, nothing more. He said if I was uncomfortable with him meeting her, he wouldn't go. Of course, I was uncomfortable with it.

I told him "No I don't want you to go."

He gave me his word that we were fine and there was no need to worry. He also told me he would cancel with her. So once again, I let it go.

But a man who commits adultery lacks judgment; whoever does so destroys himself. Proverbs 6:32 (NIV)

Now in 1999, Tom and I were home with our 3rd son. Early one morning, the home phone rang. When I answered, a man wanted to know if I was married to Tom. "Yes," I told him.

He continued to say. I want to let you know your husband is having an affair with my wife.

"Wait what?" I did not know what he was talking about.

He continued, "The affair has been going on for some time." His words surprised me, causing me to hang up the phone on him.

That evening, I once again confronted Tom with the information that I had been told. He said I have been helping this woman. He explained he had met her on the computer in a game that he played to give himself a break from work. Tom told me she was in an abusive relationship, and he was just trying to support her by giving her a shoulder to cry on. She needs to get away from her husband, he told me. She doesn't know what he could do to her. He was just doing the Christian thing and helping her by giving her counseling.

"Don't you want me to help others he replied?" "Jesus would do it." He knew I wouldn't say much about that.

Now you could say at this point that I am just refusing to see what was directly before me. Or perhaps I am so naïve and stupid that I can't see what is in front of me. I knew in my gut that he was cheating and had been for years. But I had three little boys at home and no job. He made me feel like I was imagining it all, that I was exaggerating what people had told me. I doubted my ability to know what the truth was.

Over time, as the relationship progresses, the narcissists will shift their attention to another strategy of emotional manipulation, known as trauma bonding. The narcissist will create situations that make their partner feel reliant on them for emotional, financial, and physical support. They will create a sense of fear, guilt, and obligation. They use trauma bonding as a means of creating a kind of emotional dependency, where the partner feels incapable of leaving the relationship. There are seven stages of Trauma Bonding: love bombing, getting you hooked and gaining your trust, shifting to criticism and devaluation, gaslighting, resignation, and submission, loss of a sense of self, and emotional addiction. (Those who do not know what a trauma bond is don't realize that the biggest problem with a trauma bond relationship is that the victim becomes trapped in a toxic relationship and will not leave. Especially in terms of emotional abuse, the toxicity in the relationship may be more subtle.) banyanmentalhealth.com

---

I had been praying for God to show me the truth, and he was. Why wasn't I listening to him? The problem isn't that God isn't or doesn't want to speak to me. The problem is that I'm not putting myself in the position to hear. This is how many people listen to God's word. They will hear, but they are reluctant to obey.

For the last ten years, Tom had quietly been destroying my self-image. The constant criticism that I had to endure over time gradually chipped away at my confidence until there was barely any left. Tom belittled me and told me I was not smart enough, diminishing my sense of self-worth even further. I found myself caught in a pattern of self-doubt and pessimism, certain that I was undeserving of love and had no value.

The mere thought of Tom caused me to feel nauseous and uneasy. My heartbeat was fast in my chest as I stayed silent, not wanting to talk about my marriage. The thought of my family uncovering the truth made me shudder. I just stayed in my darkness, feeling the weight of it crushing my spirit. The act of verbalizing my doubts about his loyalty could bring to light the truth that I have been hiding in the depths of my heart. I assumed that if I just kept it to myself, it would eventually go away.

If my family ever found out, they would never forgive him. Suddenly, I felt I needed to protect him. I didn't want people to assume he was a bad person, because I thought I was the one in the wrong.

It felt like God was punishing me. I didn't know why; I had always tried to be a good Christian. All I knew was I was praying every day for God to help me. My grief blinded me and I didn't see how he was trying to show me the truth.

When you are in an abusive relationship. Your abuser wants you to stay confused, they want to keep your reality in a fog. They want to convince you that you're lucky to have them. That you aren't lovable, and you'd be crazy to leave them.

A serial cheater is an individual who habitually engages in infidelity or cheating multiple times, in one or multiple relationships, showing no signs of remorse or guilt. While people may cheat in relationships for various reasons, serial cheaters have an insatiable need for external validation and attention, which they fulfill by cheating on their partners.

These individuals are often charming and charismatic, and they utilize these traits to attract and seduce multiple partners. Serial cheaters have no loyalty to any partner and are often expert liars who can weave complex webs of deceit to cover their tracks. They are typically narcissistic and have an inflated sense of self-importance, believing that their needs and desires are more important than anyone else's.

Some signs of a Serial Cheater.

They act as if nothing is ever their fault.

Overly flirty behavior cannot be denied.

They are incredibly selfish and self-absorbed.

Friends may hint that your partner is a serial cheater.

You get a bad gut feeling.

They have a habit of lying.

———————————

By all appearances, Tom was a great dad; he was so involved in everything. Every morning, he would wake up early and make bottles for me for the day. He would change diapers. He would take care of our kids without even having to be asked. Tom would go to all the doctor's appointments, and when the boys started school, he went to every parent-teacher conference from pre-school up. He attended every school function. He was involved in every part of their lives. Seeing how much Tom loved those boys made me love him even more.

Train a child in the way he should go, and when he is old, he will not turn from it. Proverbs 22:6 (NIV)

Chapter 4

The stronghold and control to manipulate

Abuse isn't always visible where someone can see it on you. It comes in many forms, but it all hurts the same. Abuse can start subtle, and you don't even realize that it is happening to you. Abuse leaves deep wounds that the power of Jesus Christ can only heal.

The trauma bonding and love bombing techniques used by narcissists are only part of the picture. Some many other signs and behaviors can indicate the presence of a narcissistic personality in a relationship. These include:

Extreme self-absorption.*A narcissist is extremely self-absorbed, and they are likely to only care about their interests.*

Lack of empathy.*A narcissist's lack of empathy means that they are incapable of recognizing other people have their own needs and can only see them solely as extensions of themselves.*

Will not take criticism.*A narcissist will not take criticism well, even if it is meant to be constructive or helpful.*

Exaggerated sense of self-importance.*A narcissist may over-inflate their achievements, needs, or abilities to feel better about themselves.*

Constant need for attention. *A narcissist constantly seeks out attention, admiration from others, and affirmation regarding their achievements.*

Difficulty maintaining relationships. *Narcissists often find it difficult to maintain long-term relationships and friendships. They may find that their friends and family members begin to avoid them over time due to emotionally abusive behavior.*

(Rage. *This is a fit of intense, furious anger that comes out of nowhere, usually over nothing (remember the wire hanger scene from the movie Mommie Dearest). It startles and shocks the victim into compliance or silence.)* psychcentral.com

(Gaslighting. *Narcissistic mental abusers lie about the past, making their victims doubt their memory, perception, and sanity. They claim and give evidence of her past wrong behavior, further causing doubt. She might even begin to question what she said a minute ago.)* quora.com

(The Stare. *This is an intense stare with no feeling behind it. It is designed to scare a victim into submission and is frequently mixed with the silent treatment.)* psychcentral.com

(Silent Treatment. *Narcissists punish by ignoring. Then they let their victim off the hook by demanding an apology, even though she isn't to blame. This is to modify her behavior. They also have a history of cutting others out of their life permanently over small things.)* athensreview.com

Projection. *They dump their issues onto their victim as if they were the ones doing it. For instance, narcissistic mental abusers may*

accuse their spouses of lying when they are the ones that had lied. Or they make her feel guilty when he is the one guilty. This creates confusion.

*(**Twisting.** When narcissistic spouses are confronted, they will twist it around to blame their victims for their actions. They will not accept responsibility for their behavior and insist that their victim apologizes to them.)* calendar-australia.com

*(**Manipulation.** A favorite manipulation tactic is for the narcissist to make their spouse fear the worst, such as abandonment, infidelity, or rejection. Then they refute it and ask her for something she normally would reply with No. This is a control tactic to get her to agree to do something she wouldn't.)* psychcentral.com

*(**Victim Card.** When all else fails, the narcissist resorts to playing the victim card. This is designed to gain sympathy and further control behavior.)* psychcentral.com

In 2001, we moved Four and a half hours north of where we lived in Oklahoma. I never had felt so alone. Tom had been up there already for about 10 months before we sold our house, and I could go with the boys. I was in a new town, knowing no one.

Tom was working more than ever. He was rarely at home because of his busy schedule and other commitments. Frequently, there were discrepancies in his paycheck, as it did not reflect the total amount of overtime he had worked. I would question him about it. Of course, he would always have an excuse.

Sometimes he would just talk circles around me, getting me all confused about the hours he worked. The issue wasn't that he worked late nights, but rather that they did not compensate him for it. He never seemed to mind that he was being shorted.

I would get down on my knees and pray that God would lift my burden, put his angels around me, and just show me what I couldn't see. Once again, God started to move and tell me what to do, even when I didn't understand.

What do you do when you don't know what to do? How can we discern if it's our will or God's? And how do we do the right thing—what seems to be God's leading but seems so wrong? This scripture helped me decide:

Trust in the Lord with all your heart and lean not on your own understanding; in all your ways acknowledge him, and he will make your paths straight. Proverbs 3: 5-6 (NIV)

This was about the time that the internet was becoming popular. The warnings were coming out about your kids being on the internet and what they could get into. I saw a TV program that showed how you could look up a name in a search engine to find out which websites they had signed up for. A feeling of urgency came over me, telling me to investigate Tom. I couldn't explain why I had this urge to do that, yet the feeling wouldn't disappear. So, I decided to just try it. I typed Tom's name and hit the search bar. I sat there in shock, looking at what was on the screen. There was a dating site in the local area that had Tom's name on it. I wanted to scream, punch something, and tear something up! What in the world was happening? What was he thinking? When I talked to him about it, he blew it off by saying,

"Oh, that is nothing." He claimed it was a website he had found to make new friends so he would not get depressed being in a new city without his family. He told me I didn't know what it was like being in an unfamiliar city all alone. I replied.

"Well, I clicked on your profile and the only friends that you are making are women."

He got furious with me, was very defensive, and then just stared at me without talking. If you ever challenged him on anything that he said, he no longer wanted to talk about it. He would just give me the blank facial stare and silent treatment. I just had become numb to my life at this point.

He had lived ten months in this new town without us. I am unaware of what he did during that time and likely won't ever find out.

Those who work their land will have abundant food, but those who chase fantasies have lacks judgment. Proverbs 12:11 (NIV)

I believe I mentioned it before. My family is very dear to me, and we are extremely close. Living three and a half hours away from them made it hard for me. I tried to take the boys back as often as I could. Usually, every spring break, we would spend time back home with our family where I grew up. We always went back during the summer for a week while the fair was going on.

The children always treasured those times. Tom was usually working and would never go with us. Typically, after returning home after a wonderful week being with family. Tom would say things to me like,

"After you spend time with your family, I must train you all over again."

Then laughed like he was making a joke. I didn't find any humor in it. He meant every word.

The effects of emotional abuse can be short-term to long-term. You can suffer from self-image problems, mental health concerns, and even physical effects. When you start feeling isolated, powerless, or worthless in your relationships, you need to pay closer attention. Notably, a narcissistic relationship can be extremely damaging to the individual, both physically and emotionally. Narcissistic behaviors can lead to depression, anxiety, low self-worth, and feelings of helplessness, even in previously strong individuals. This can lead to long-term emotional trauma that may take years to overcome with the right treatment.

Although the situation was less than ideal, we could still make a good impression. To the outside world, we had the perfect family. We would always put on our Sunday best and our smiles. Nobody knew what was happening behind closed doors. Tom continued to have a Jekyll and Hyde personality. He could be extremely nice and just downright lovable, then out of the blue for no reason, he could become very harsh.

No matter what I planned for us to do, it always seemed to be the wrong choice. His behavior made it impossible to enjoy any activity he was a part of. He consistently left the decision-making to me, whether it was about where we should dine, what activities we could engage in for the evening, or the movie we could watch. However, once I decided, he was never happy with it. He found fault in every decision that I made. This made me very insecure about wanting to decide because I did not want the misery of being wrong. I always gave great thought to whatever we were going to do because I had no intention of making him mad. This alone broke me in ways that I cannot describe. I lost myself, you could say. I no longer knew what I liked or didn't like to do. To this very day, I struggle with deciding for fear of making the wrong one.

Have you ever had that sickening feeling in the pit of your stomach every time you needed to talk to someone? Especially about something that you knew would be uncomfortable and could make them mad. This was me almost every day. I would do my best to not have to communicate with Tom regarding anything serious because I did not know what his reaction would be. There could be days we didn't even speak to each other.

I noticed he had this behavior with our boys as well. But I would not have that! I stepped into taking the brunt of his ranting. This way, the boys did not have to endure his wrath.

(The gut-brain connection makes it possible for emotional experiences to register as gastrointestinal distress.) healthline.com *We get this feeling because the narcissist wants to confuse, disappoint, frustrate, and hurt you. Your gut hates it and is informing you what's happening to you. Living under these conditions doesn't affect the relationship partner momentarily rather, it's a slow and vicious cycle that eats away at a person's self-esteem, emotional capacity, and mental health.*

As the boys got older and became involved with sports and boy scouts, Tom continued to be very involved in their lives. He went to every practice or game that they had, and he would try to give them pointers on their sport. He became a leader in the Boy Scouts and took them camping once a month. Tom worked hours helping our boys to become Eagle Scouts. I had great hope he was changing. But if we disagreed, he would tell me things like,

I wasn't a good parent, or I wasn't raising my boys correctly.

He would just say these things to be hurtful, and they did.

Indeed, I am not perfect, but I am constantly working to improve myself. It became clear to me that certain aspects of my life needed improvement and I will work on them.

I believed that if I could give Tom more attention, our relationship would improve, and he would feel happier with me. Maybe if I made better meals and kept the house cleaner, he would like to be at home more. Upon reflection, I am not entirely convinced that those actions would have had any impact.

I started putting it all together. The times that Tom would be angry and not speak to me, and the times he would make me feel like everything I did was wrong. I feel like these were the periods that he had another woman. The weeks that he was nice, we got along, and had a good time were the weeks he didn't have someone on the side.

(A serial cheater is not seeking love or a relationship, but attention and power.) Joannalipari.medium.com *Serial cheaters cannot stop cheating because they have developed a behavioral addiction to cheating. This addiction, like any other addiction, can be hard to break unless the individual seeks help to overcome it. Serial cheating can be linked to a condition called sex addiction, a psychological addiction that leads to compulsive sexual behavior.*

Another reason why serial cheaters cannot stop cheating is that they lack the ability to form meaningful emotional connections. They tend to use sex as a means of validating their self-worth, and they are much more interested in the thrill of the chase than in developing meaningful emotional bonds. Ultimately, they find it easier to cheat rather than put in the emotional work required to make a relationship work.

Chapter 5

The hope of a new start

In 2008, when the economy hit an all-time low, Tom lost his job. He came home and told me he no longer wanted to do the type of work he had been doing for the last 30 years. Tom expressed to me his desire to go back to school to become a Respiratory Therapist. My initial reaction to this idea was overwhelmingly positive, as I thought it was a great one. It is possible that this was a new beginning for us, marking a fresh start in our lives. By embracing change and being open-minded, we can welcome new experiences that could have a profound impact on our lives. If we work towards our goals together, we can not only improve our financial situation but also strengthen our relationship and grow closer to each other.

One thing that I failed to consider when he started attending school was the numerous young, attractive, slim, and intelligent girls on campus. There would be many study dates and countless evenings in the school library. This would be right up his alley.

But I tell you that anyone who looks at a woman lustfully has already committed adultery with her in his heart. Matthew 5:28 (NIV)

After a while of being in school, Tom needed to start clinical in the hospitals. He would go on and on about how he did not like anyone in his class. They are all so young and don't have their lives together. He went over the top, telling me how glad he would be when he didn't have to be around all of them anymore.

Something seemed off to me. I snooped around for anything I could find. Whenever he needed to use the bathroom, he would usually forget to bring his phone with him. I picked it up and proceeded to go through it.

I took the initiative to learn how to hack into his email on my own. I'm not proud of that fact, nor am I proud that I even made-up emails pretending to be women he worked with at the hospitals. I sent him those emails to observe his response. Well, he responded just the way I thought he would. He wanted to meet for coffee to get to know each other better. Additionally, I uncovered some text messages during my investigation, which revealed that he was engaging in flirting and sweet talking with some girls in his class. The situation was challenging, but I was able to keep my cool and stay in control. I just kept telling myself it was not true.

Is being nice and talking to other women considered cheating? He kept telling me it wasn't.

I found myself in a state of confusion, unable to distinguish between what was true and what I should believe.

There were times when my thoughts were so overwhelming that I thought I might lose my grip on reality. Was what I felt like Tom was doing being made up in my head?

I decided I needed to go buy a three-ring binder where I could start keeping track of all the information I discovered. Right here is where I documented the names and phone numbers of the women I found out he was communicating with. I put the emails between Tom and the other women that I had printed off in there as well. Along with the phone records. I kept track of everything.

This helped me a little from feeling as though I was going insane.

To compound the situation and make it worse. Tom would spend money beyond our means and cause significant financial strain on our family. He would compulsively buy anything he wanted, disregarding any responsibility to live within our financial means.

This made me feel frustrated, overwhelmed, and often helpless to keep up with the unrealistic financial demands. It left me to figure out how to make ends meet, sometimes taking extreme measures to avoid financial distress. Tom showed no remorse, empathy, or understanding regarding his irresponsible behavior, and instead blamed me for our financial shortcomings.

The effects of verbal and emotional abuse can be devastating, leading to significant negative impacts on the mental health, self-esteem, and overall well-being of the victim. Victims of emotional and verbal abuse may experience depression, anxiety, feelings of shame, and low self-worth, and may struggle in their daily lives, such as in their career and social relationships. The abusive behaviors can also escalate into physical abuse, which can cause physical injury, trauma, and even death.

It is essential to recognize the signs of emotional and verbal abuse and to speak out against them, no matter who the abuser is. Victims of abuse should seek support from friends, family, or a professional therapist, as breaking free from the cycle of abuse can be incredibly challenging. It is important to address the abuse to prevent it from continuing and to begin the healing process.

I knew I needed to talk to someone. I wanted someone to tell me I wasn't crazy. A friend of mine told me they had a counselor at their church that I should reach out to and talk with her about my marriage and how Tom was treating me. My initial impression was that this idea was a good one. I did not know of them, and they had no information about me. So, they wouldn't tell anyone I knew about me coming in to see them. I called and made an appointment with the counselor.

After sitting in her office and visiting with her about my life, I walked out of there more confused than ever. She did not give me any advice on what I should do, or if what he was doing was adultery.

I merely sought clarification if what he was doing was wrong. Or was I just overreacting, like he always told me I was? Did I have grounds for divorce in God's eyes?

I have learned that not all Christian counselors are pure. It is important that your counselor shares your faith and integrate biblical and psychological principles. Filters all treatment through the lens of Scripture. Follow the Holy Spirit's guidance will listen to you and pray for you.

For from within, out of men's hearts, come evil thoughts, sexual immorality, theft, murder, adultery. Mark 7:21 (NIV)

Serial cheaters have a distorted sense of their own identity and feel a sense of power and control over others when they cheat. They believe they are above the rules and that they can get away with anything they do. This sense of power and control over others only reinforces their addiction to cheating and makes them feel invincible.

Serial cheating leads to many negative consequences. It can destroy any trust and emotional connection in a relationship, resulting in feelings of betrayal, guilt, anger, and depression. The constant need for external validation and attention can also lead to a dependence on cheating, which can have devastating consequences for the individual's mental and social health.

Over the next couple of years, Tom started pulling away from the church. It did not take long at all for him to stop going all together to church with us. For a while, I would plead with him to go with us. But he started saying things to me like,

"Oh, you are the church lady now."

I've got to be honest, the Sunday mornings he pretended to be asleep in bed and wouldn't get up and go with us. I started not to be sad about that at all. It was easier for me if he would stay home and not go. Because it was becoming increasingly difficult for me to maintain the façade that everything was fine. So, I found myself hoping and praying that he would stay asleep and not get up and go with us.

There are a variety of reasons why an individual may turn away from the church, such as experiencing a

dramatic life change, or it could be that they are fully aware of their actions and are choosing to live a life of sin.

We finally made it through his two years of school. His class was going to have a party on a Saturday night, but he informed me it was for students only. They did not invite spouses. That was the silliest thing I had ever heard. I asked him if I could come, anyway? Tom simply said,

"No, you can't."

I reminded him how he didn't like any of his classmates, and why he would want to spend time with them. He just blew me off. As he was shutting the door he said,

"I won't be late."

He left the house around 5 p.m. By midnight, I started calling him. His phone went right to voice mail. He did not return home until 4 a.m. the next morning. I was beside myself, just wondering what or who he was with. The following morning Tom just indicated that they all were just having a fun time and he lost all track of time. He claimed his phone went dead, and he had no way of charging it. The words that he spoke to me did not seem truthful, and I found it hard to believe them. I reached the last straw. I had finally had enough. Tom had to be made aware that I was serious. I knew I needed to leave Tom. But I had to be clever in how I did this. I tried to keep my family and the boys in the dark about the situation. Desperately, I was looking for a way to restore the relationship I had with Tom.

I made up my mind to inform Tom that I'm leaving him and heading back to my hometown. Maybe this would scare him into changing how he was behaving and realize how much he loved me.

I needed a story to tell my family why I wanted to come home. I called my brother and asked if he had any work I could do for his company. I came up with the story that I was hoping Tom would get a job there when he was done with school. And I hoped to come back early to get my youngest son in school before summer so he could start making friends. Fortunately, my brother had some work available for me to do.

Wasting no time, I quickly dialed my mother's number on my phone and asked if they could accommodate the boys and me until Tom finished school. Without a doubt, the answer to the question was a resounding yes. So, in one short week, I informed Tom I was leaving him. I packed up and went back home. I was careful not to say anything that would let anyone know our situation.

Tom begged me not to go, and it devastated him. He promised to do better. I felt like he needed to know I was serious and would not put up with him acting like that anymore.

I was back with my parents for four months. Tom would just plead for me to return home. Tom made it a point to call every day and express how strong his love was and how much he missed me. He would tell me he was planning to make things right between us. We were going to have a good life together. He wanted me to come home.

Future faking is grand promises of a future that the manipulator has no intention of keeping. Instead, they distort reality to get what they want form you now.

After a few months had passed, I believed that he had finally comprehended the gravity of my seriousness. My love for him persisted despite our separation, and I had a strong conviction that I wouldn't be able to handle life without him. So, I was thrilled he was going to change.

Love bombing is a manipulative and controlling tactic often used by abusive and narcissistic individuals to gain control over their partners. The goal of love bombing is to create an intense emotional bond, so the victim becomes dependent on the abuser. However, these grand displays of affection are rarely genuine and are used as a tool to gain control over the victim. Abusers may use this tactic to escalate the relationship quickly or get their partner to forgive or overlook abusive behavior. Despite the intense emotional surge, love bombing is a form of manipulation, and victims should be aware of the tactics used to establish control over them. It is essential to seek help from professionals to recognize and break the pattern of abuse.

I desperately wanted to move back home. I informed my family that Tom had been denied the job there. But he had been offered a job at the hospital where he had done clinical work, which would be much better for us. So, unfortunately, I would go back home.

Trauma bonding is a psychological response to repeated abuse or trauma, and it can manifest itself as an intense, emotional bond with an abuser. This bond often relies on a push-and-pull dynamic,

He started working at that hospital full-time shortly after he graduated. It was an excellent job and a huge blessing to come along when we needed it so badly. Unfortunately, Tom got sick, we found out he had kidney cancer. The benefits of working for the hospital were they paid all our medical bills. Which was amazing! He was in the hospital for a couple of weeks. He didn't seem to want me up there with him very often. Before the night shift began, he wanted me to have left already. That was the shift he worked. (That should have been a clue). After he got back on his feet, he continued working for that hospital for another eight months. Then one day Tom came home and told me they had fired him. His explanation was he didn't give one of his patients the right treatment. My gut was all worked up. I felt that wasn't true. He refused to budge from that story. My curiosity got the best of me, and I had to discover what the truth was. Although I didn't know how. After a period, the truth finally came to light. I discovered they had caught him with a nurse in the storage room.

Marriage should be honored by all, and the marriage bed kept pure, for God will judge the adulterer and all the sexually immoral. Hebrews 13:4 (NIV)

We were not sure what we should do now. Although Tom was considering other job offers, he ultimately accepted a position with a traveling healthcare company. I was pleasantly surprised by the pay offered for this job. I must say that it was truly excellent. In my opinion, the idea was a great one, and I was fully supportive of it. We worked on getting him licensed in several states. It didn't dawn on me. He would be away from us and could do anything he wanted without me knowing. His first assignment was three hours away from our home, which meant he would stay there for about three months before the job would finish. After he was gone for a couple of weeks. I believed I was having a breakdown. I had reached a point where I felt completely helpless and unable to pick up the pieces of my life, as I felt like I was broken beyond repair.

Discovering all of his activities and knowing whom he was speaking to became an all-consuming obsession for me. There was an intense feeling of curiosity inside of me that was almost too much to handle. I spent my days sifting through whatever I could find to learn about my husband's activity. Being so confused; I believed I might go crazy. Feeling powerless to stop the momentum I had created. I decided I would do everything I could to find out what he was doing. I went and bought spyware to put on his laptop computer. This way, I could see everything he did on it. Now I had his password to his emails and could log in to see whom he was emailing. Signing into our cell phone account is something I could do too. This way I could tell who he was texting and talking to. I'm not sure where I picked up those skills, but I knew what to do. I had become proficient in looking up phone numbers to determine who the accounts belonged to. There was one number that came up a lot on our account while he was gone. Finding out it was a woman he worked with; he was talking with her at all hours every night. I just came right out and asked him why he was talking with this woman. His response was they were talking about Jesus. He claimed she wasn't a Christian, and he was leading her to Christ.

"Are you kidding me?" I asked.

Tom hadn't gone to church in years and was not living a Christian lifestyle, so how could he lead anyone to Christ?

———————

The Bible is clear on the consequences of being a false teacher or using Jesus to hide one's sin. In **Matthew 7:15-20 (NIV)** Jesus warns his follower's to. **Watch out for false prophets. They come to you in sheep's clothing, but inwardly they are ferocious wolves. By their fruit, you will recognize them. Do people pick grapes from thornbushes or figs from thistles? Likewise, every good tree bears good fruit, but a bad tree bears bad fruit. A good tree cannot bear bad fruit, and a bad tree cannot bear good fruit. Every tree that does not bear good fruit is cut down and thrown into the fire. Thus, by their fruit, you will recognize them.**

In other words, false teachers may appear to be good and holy on the surface, but their teachings and actions will ultimately reveal their true character. Similarly, in **1 John 1:6-7 (NIV)** the apostle John warns against claiming to have fellowship with God while still walking in darkness. He writes, **If we claim to have fellowship with him and yet walk in the darkness, we lie and do not live out the truth. But if we walk in the light, as he is in the light, we have fellowship with one another, and the blood of Jesus, his Son, purifies us from all sin.** Jesus cannot be used as a cover for sin, and those who attempt to do so are living a lie. Ultimately, the truth will be revealed, and those who persist in hiding their sin behind the name of Jesus will face the consequences of their actions.

Chapter 6

The fire destroyed more than our home

The boys and I were unfortunate enough to face a house fire while Tom was out-of-town for work, which was a very scary and difficult experience. I cannot put the extent of the devastation that occurred into words. It was truly heart-wrenching. Unfortunately, a significant portion of our belongings were lost. Dealing with the aftermath of a fire can be a daunting task, as it often involves extensive cleanup and rebuilding efforts. Once we were able to return to our home, the smell that lingered from the fire was so overpowering that it was even stronger than the scent of a campfire. We walked around the area in darkness with no electricity and with wet floors caused by the water used by the firefighters. Black streaks that ran down from the ceiling to the floor marred the walls.

With no clear direction or starting point, it left me feeling bewildered and unsure about what to do. Thanks to the insurance company, we could live in an apartment in the same town while our home was being repaired. This way, the boys could still go to school.

Tom came home every few weeks to check on how I was progressing in all the work that needed to be done. The insurance provider advised us to write down every item in the house, the cost we bought it for, and the cost to replace it. This alone took the boys and me six months to complete. I sat in one room at a time. The boys would bring me an item, I would write it down, and they would haul it to the dumpster outside.

I would ask Tom to come home and help us, and he simply replied.

"It's your fault we had a fire, therefore you can be the one to fix it."

I finished with all the material stuff for the home. Then I became the general contractor for redoing the dwelling, trying to save us money where I could. It took us almost two years to rebuild and re-buy everything for our home.

Tom traveled to a lot of places during those two years. I tried going to a few of these places with the boys, making it like a family vacation.

When the boys and I could move back into our home, they had just assigned Tom to a new town for his job, way out west in our state. He seemed to like this place a lot. He told me he would stay there for as long as they wanted him to.

I, once again, became very obsessed with looking through phone records and emails. I needed to know what Tom was up to. Looking at our phone records, there was always one phone number that appeared over and over again in their records.

I needed a friend, someone I could trust, and someone that knew some of our past. I called my old friend Nancy; she was the one that told me about Tom meeting his ex-fiancé. I hadn't talked to her in quite a while. So, I filled her in on what had happened over the past few years. I told her I was concerned about this recent phone number that kept coming up on his phone records. She asked if I wanted her to call the number. Oh yes, I did, I really did! I gave her the phone number, and she called it. Just a few short minutes later, she called me back. She informed me a woman answered and said her name was Kelly.

"Was this ever going to stop?" I asked!

My friend Nancy simply said, "Gina, you are an abused woman.

" I am NOT, I exclaimed!

Tom has never hit me. She informed me there are other types of abuse besides physical. She explained that there is mental and emotional suffering, and Tom has inflicted both on me. "You are an abused woman, and you need to get some counseling," she replied. I just couldn't accept that. It has taken me years to accept the fact that I am an abused woman. Tom had taught me how to act and to love him, but it still wasn't enough for him.

For you created my inmost being; you knit me together in my mother's womb. I praise you because I am fearfully and wonderfully made; your works are wonderful; I know that full well. Psalm 139: 13-14 (NIV)

(Emotional abuse is more common in relationships, as people tend to overlook it. It is the most pervasive form of relationship maltreatment because it can be subtle, insidious, and manipulative. Separation may seem like the most obvious choice in an abusive relationship, but it isn't always so easy. Women often have limited resources to live independently, and with children and families involved, they are often forced to continue living in abusive

To fix things in my marriage. I thought we needed a real family vacation together. It was a priority for me that Tom had quality time with us. I didn't aspire to be the one that had to make all the decisions and then be wrong. I figured a cruise would be the best for us. That way, I wouldn't have to choose where to eat every night, what activities to participate in, or the places we would visit. The solution was perfect and exactly what we needed. We made our plans and went on to what I wished would be an ideal vacation.

My expectations were met and even exceeded as everything turned out, just as I had hoped it would. The boys had so much fun. We even met who would later become my future daughter-in-law on this cruise. Everyone was having a blast! Everyone except Tom. His afternoons were spent napping in the boy's cabin. He didn't seem angry; he was just distant. Our cruise finally ended, but I didn't feel any better about my marriage.

After returning home from our vacation. Tom told me he had slept with a woman in the town he had just come from. Her name was Kelly and he worked with her at the hospital.

An instant rage came over me. I began hitting him. I couldn't control myself. He insisted it was a one-time thing, and that he had made a huge mistake. During our conversation, he expressed his overwhelming sense of guilt to me. That was the reason for his distance on our cruise. He promised he would not do that again. I yelled at him to get out, then I fell to the floor.

This was the first time Tom had ever said the words,

"I slept with another woman."

The words coming out of his mouth made it all real. My life was now over. What was I going to do?

Later that night we had a very hard conversation, and I told him I wanted him to go get tested for sexual diseases. I insisted that because he had been sleeping with someone, she could have given him something. He argued with me, telling me saying she had nothing. How was I to know this? I made it clear to him that his actions were unfair, and that completing this task would help soothe my mind. He rejected the idea of going to the doctor and refused to be tested. In a few days, he would travel back to the same town to continue his work. He was going to be back to her.

As he was leaving, he looked right into my eyes and said he would never sleep with anyone again.

The phrase "once a cheater, always a cheater" is widely accepted. Nevertheless, it is a common occurrence that individuals who have engaged in cheating on numerous occasions may not be able to break free from their cheating tendencies.

After he was gone, I woke up one morning. It became apparent to me I needed help. I wanted to go to counseling. But the last time I went to counseling, it did not go as well as I had hoped. So, I was a little hesitant to go again.

I decided to contact my pastor to find out if I could come to see him and discuss something with him. I knew I could trust him. That next morning, I went in and told him everything! I dumped my complete life story before him. He could sense my brokenness. He asked if I wanted to fix my marriage. And I did. I wanted it all to be fixed. He told me he would talk to and counsel Tom.

He put me with three ladies in the church. These three ladies had some training in counseling and the pastor thought they could help me. I went home and called Tom. I asked him if he wanted to save our marriage. He needed to do this counseling with the pastor. He agreed and said he would do anything. Tom told me he would give the pastor a call and set everything up with him.

The very next day, I started meeting with the ladies. They gave me a book we were going to read through. They prayed with me and just listened to me. I had faith that this would help me. Tom was away but could do his sessions via Skype.

For lack of guidance a nation falls, but many advisers make victory sure. Proverbs 11:14 (NIV)

*L*earning *to trust again after a betrayal can be a challenging and painful process, but it is possible with effort and patience. The first step is to acknowledge and process the hurt, betrayal, and trauma that caused the lack of trust. It's important to allow yourself* *to grieve and feel your emotions without judgment. Then you must re-engage with your partner or others by communicating your feelings and establishing clear boundaries. It's also important to take time and heal on your terms, reflect on your vulnerabilities and ways that trust was violated to identify areas of personal growth. With transparency, commitment, honesty, and time, it is possible to rebuild trust and have healthy relationships again.*

I still felt very anxious and uncomfortable about Tom's interactions with other women. Not knowing if he had contracted a sexually transmitted disease and had passed it on to me. After a great deal of hesitation, I eventually decided to call my doctor and set up an appointment for myself.

Taking a deep breath, I walked into the office and sat in the chair, waiting to see my doctor. I felt humiliated with the doctor standing in front of me asking why I was in today. I had to look her in her eyes and say,

"I need to be tested for sexual diseases."

She wanted to know if there were any specific things that I wanted to be tested for.

I didn't even know what kinds there were. Tears going down my cheeks, I simply replied,

"I have only been with one man in 27 years. I think I need to be tested for everything there is." "

I understand," she said, "I will take care of it."

It was a shameful experience for me to be there doing that. Going through such an experience should never be something that anyone must do. For as long as I live, I never wish to be in that situation again.

D*on't hesitate to Get Tested!*
Getting tested for STDs might be the last thing you want to think about or deal with after your partner has cheated on you. However, you should make your health a priority, and this is an essential part of doing so.

Chapter 7

The truth shall set you free

When we fall on our knees and ask God to help us, he will. He might not always answer us in the ways we want. And sometimes we don't understand the answers he is giving us. But God will answer your prayers in his way and timing.

As an emotionally and verbally abused woman of a cheating husband, it may seem like there is no escape from the pain and turmoil you are experiencing. But the Bible is filled with promises of God's protection and support, even when all seems lost. In **Psalm 91:11-12 (NIV) For he will command his angels concerning you to guard you in all your ways; they will lift you up in their hands, so that you will not strike your foot against a stone.** These verses remind us that God is always watching over us, and he sends his angels to protect and guard us in times of trouble.

We are promised that God will never leave us or forsake us. In **Hebrews 13:5-6 (NIV) Keep your lives free from the love of money and be content with what you have, because God has said, "Never will I leave you; never will I forsake you." "The Lord is my helper; I will not be afraid. What can man do to me?"** Therefore, even in the midst of a difficult and abusive situation, we can take comfort in the knowledge that God is with us and will never abandon us. He will send his angels to protect us and give us the strength to persevere. With the help of God's angels, we can find the courage to seek help and escape from an abusive situation.

What I am about to tell you, I sometimes don't believe it myself. The only explanation I have for it is GOD was working so hard to save me in any way he could. If sending me an angel to protect me from Tom was the only way, then he was going to do exactly that.

Then you will know the truth, and the truth will set you free. John 8:32 (NIV)

One afternoon while cleaning the house, I got a text asking me a question about something. I can't even remember what the question was now. I replied,

"I am sorry you have the wrong number."

The individual on the other side of the line answered,

"I'm sorry."

Then, they just started making conversation with me. I was polite and answered their questions. I had nothing else to do. Over the next few weeks, they texted me quite a bit. I know this sounds funny and a little suspicious, but I felt very comfortable with this stranger at the other end of my phone. I opened up to them. There was something about being able to talk to someone that didn't know me, my family, or anything about me. They only knew what I told them. Taking extra precautions, I made sure not to give them too much information. I didn't provide them with any information about our identities or the location of our residence. Just to be safe, I wanted to make sure I was protecting myself in case they happened to be mentally unhinged. Although I spilled out everything about me and my marriage.

We chatted for about 3 months. This stranger was understanding and gave me good advice. In addition, I updated them that I was undergoing counseling sessions to work on my marriage and that I was feeling positive and hopeful about the current state of things. I believed in my heart Tom was doing all the hard work as well. I was confident that we could move forward and put this awful time in our marriage behind us.

But if the unbeliever leaves, let him do so. A believing man or woman is not bound in such circumstances; God has called us to live in peace. 1 Corinthians 7:15 (NIV)

Right before Christmas, I had gone to the store to start my weekly grocery shopping. When my phone beeped and I looked at the screen, I saw I had received a text from my mystery friend. The text that I saw had the words,

"What if he isn't?"

The text went on to say,

"What if he is playing you as a fool and isn't changing? What if he is still cheating?"

I became mad.

"Are you trying to make me feel like my marriage will not work?" I asked.

The text continued, "What if I can prove he is still cheating?"

I stated, "How can you do that? You don't even know who we are?"

Then, in one sentence, my world came crashing down. The text read,

"Gina, I know for a fact Tom is still sleeping with Kelly."

I couldn't get out of the store fast enough. My mind went blank. I started shaking. Who have I been talking to? Was this a stalker? How did they know our names? What did they want from me? All I wanted to do was get home. After pulling into my drive, sitting in my car, I picked up the phone. I needed to know who this was and what they wanted from me. My heart was beating fast. When I dialed the number, I was greeted by a pleasant elderly man. He said,

"Hi, Gina."

As tears filled my eyes, I asked,

"Who are you?"

He explained. My name is Sam. I know who you are because of your husband. Well, that sent me into a frantic fit. My mind went straight to Tom. Was he setting me up?

Sam continued to tell me he actually knew Kelly; the woman Tom had been sleeping with. He asked me to be patient while he explained.

"This past summer, I was on a dating site" he began saying. "A woman named Kelly started talking to me. I live in Tennessee, and she lives thirteen hundred miles away from me so, we never met but talked a lot. Then one day she just started telling me about a man at her work. She said this man was a traveling Respiratory Therapist. Kelly thought he was the hottest man she had ever met, but the only problem was that he was married. She said he was married to a dumb woman that would never know he was sleeping around. He wasn't happy in the marriage anyway, so it made the cheating alright."

Sam continued to tell me that Kelly had sent him a picture of me, just to show how foolish I looked. Kelly would just laugh, stating how stupid I was; I would never find out Tom was sleeping with her.

Then Kelly even gave him my phone number. She was the one who had been stalking me. Sam told me he took one look at me, and he had the feeling he needed to help me. He said that he could tell immediately just by my photo I was an innocent lady with a kind soul. He didn't want Tom and Kelly to make me look like a fool. However, he needed to make sure his instinct about me was true. So, he pretended to contact me accidentally.

He apologized for lying to me. He just didn't know any other way. I told him I needed a few moments to comprehend and make sense of all the information he had just given me.

As I hung up the phone, I felt like all the air had been taken out of me, leaving me completely breathless. Now I had to go inside and pretend in front of my boys that everything was alright. I continued to replay the phone call in my head all evening. I needed to know more.

After fixing supper and cleaning up the kitchen, the boys were watching TV. Making my way up to my room, I shut the door and looked around to see where I could go to call Sam back without having the boys hear me. The place I had in mind was perfect. Upon entering my closet, I flipped the light switch to illuminate the space and then closed the door firmly. After pushing the shirts to the side, I made a spot on the ground between the heaps of clothes and settled in.

I slowly called Sam back. As he picked up the phone, I just started crying. Despite my best efforts, I found myself unable to stop. I finally said,

"Please tell me more."

Sam continued,

"I don't want to hurt you, Gina. My goal is to help you see the truth. To be honest, I have done nothing like this before. I would never get involved with someone else's marriage problems. I just knew God was telling me to help you. I know this seems hard to believe. What do you need from me to let you know I am telling the truth? If you'd like, I can send you text messages from the two of them corresponding to each other. Kelly has been telling me everything that happens between them. She doesn't tell me about any other guy, just Tom. It is the weirdest thing that has ever happened to me. I can send you photos of them in bed together. She has sent some of those as well. It was like she couldn't help herself from telling me every little detail of their relationship."

I am shaking and with tears running down my face, I said,

"I believe you."

Over the next few weeks, Sam slowly revealed to me every move they made. He sent me text messages and even the photos he obtained from Kelly. I had to beg to get those because he didn't want me to see them, but I just had to see for myself.

Tom would come home for visits. I just pretended that everything was going great. I asked him about his counseling. He told me stories about how well the sessions were going. Tom would even bring home the book he was supposedly reading. He told me he read every night before he went to sleep. This left me a bit confused by the conflicting stories I was getting from Sam.

Although I could tell Tom wasn't changing, he was as mean as ever to me and the boys. As that book just sat on the nightstand, I could tell it wasn't being moved. Despite my best efforts to hold back, I couldn't help but ask him questions, which invariably led to his anger and frustration with me. I decided to investigate and establish whether he was reading this book.

Among the pages of the book, I positioned a dime right in the middle. I knew if he picked up the book, the dime would fall out. Then I would know at least if he was reading the book. A week went by. I once again asked if he was putting in the work on our marriage. He replied,

"Yes, and said you need to quit asking me that."

I walked right over to the book, turned to the page where the dime was, and it was still there right where I placed it. I let him know what I had done, and I called him a liar and a cheat. Then, I just left the room.

The next day, I called my pastor and asked if I could come in and talk to him about Tom and me. The next morning, as I was preparing to go in and visit with my pastor. I lay flat on the floor, face down, with my arms out wide at the end of my bed. I started to pray and beg God. If Tom wasn't doing what he needs to do to save our marriage, then please release me from the love, hurt, and hate that I have in my heart. Lord, if it is your will, help me let him go.

The righteous cry out, and the Lord hears them; he delivers them from all their troubles. The Lord is close to the brokenhearted and saves the crushed in spirit. A righteous man may have many troubles, but the Lord delivers him from them all, he protects all his bones, not one of them will be broken. Psalm 34:17-20 (NIV)

I walked into the church office. There sat two of the ladies I had been counseling with, as well as the pastor. I took a seat at the table. The pastor asked how I was doing. I said that I had done everything that was asked of me. It is my belief that personal growth is a continuous process and because of this I have reached a point where I can forgive Tom for his actions.

Although I hope for a change, my innermost feelings tell me that he will not change. It has come to my attention that Tom is still engaging in sexual relations with female colleagues at his place of employment. At times, he is not nice to me, or the boys, when he comes home from being gone for work.

I asked the pastor.

"Can you please tell me how many sessions he has attended?"

He said,

"I normally cannot discuss anything about Tom's counseling, but because he has done none with me, I can. Tom always misses our Skype meetings. Tom then tells me he has overslept. When I give him homework to do, like reading, he says he is just too busy to complete it. So, what I am telling you is that Tom has done nothing to better himself or to fix the marriage."

I burst into tears. As I sat there sobbing, not knowing what I was going to do.

Then all at once, I felt like a light switch inside of me was turned on. My tears suddenly dried up. All the feelings I had for him, all the love, hurt, and hate I had for him, were gone. I felt nothing. I was not angry, sad, or even mad. It was weird and amazing all at the same time.

I knew exactly what I needed to do. I needed to divorce Tom. It was January and my middle son would be graduating in May. I didn't want to do anything until his graduation. I began planning my exit.

First, I needed to tell my parents.

The consequences of a narcissistic relationship can take years to heal from. It is important to note that there is help and support available if you are experiencing a toxic relationship with a narcissist, and seeking help is the first step to healing.

Chapter 8

Leaving is never easy

The truth can be freeing. Even when it is hard to let someone know what you have been going through. The peace I have now is worth everything I've lost.

I speak the truth in Christ, I am not lying, my conscience confirms it in the Holy Spirit. Romans 9:1 (NIV)

Telling my parents was very difficult for me. It took them by surprise. They did not know that I wasn't happy. I never revealed what I was going through. And now, I still couldn't tell them everything. I wasn't ready to talk about all that had gone on in the last 27 years. My family was supportive and said they would help the boys and me in any way they could.

Sharing with your family that you are getting divorced can be one of the hardest moments of your life. However, the Bible provides comforting words for those who are going through the pain of separation. In **Matthew 19:6 (NIV)** it is written, **"So they are no longer two, but one. Therefore what God has joined together, let man not separate."** These verses remind us that marriage is a bond, and in times of divorce, one must do everything possible to preserve that union. Nevertheless, it also acknowledges that sometimes divorce is necessary, and when that happens, God will be there to comfort and guide us.

Furthermore, In **Matthew 5:32 (NIV)** Jesus specifically talks about divorce stating, **"But I tell you that anyone who divorces his wife, except for marital unfaithfulness, causes her to become an adulteress, and anyone who marries a divorced woman commits adultery".** While it's true, that divorce is not something God condones, the option is there for those who find themselves in situations that lack love and respect. Although divorce is at times necessary, God still calls us to forgiveness. **Romans 12:18 (NIV) If it is possible, as far as it depends on you, live at peace with everyone.** Forgiveness can be challenging, but it's God's intention for us to do so, as stated in **Mark 11:25 (NIV) "And when you stand praying if you hold anything against anyone, forgive them, so that your Father in heaven may forgive you your sins."**

Sam kept me posted on Tom and Kelly's every move. I would call Tom nonstop when I knew Kelly was with my husband. Or I would have the boys call their dad to interrupt their romantic night. Sam would report back to me that Kelly was wondering why I was always calling when she and Tom were together. They suspected the landlord was keeping tabs on them and letting me know when they were together. Then they decided to meet at hotels. Kelly continued to let Sam know where they were going. So, I continued to interrupt them as well. It was somewhat entertaining for me. They were so confused! At this point, I'm amazed that Kelly still couldn't help herself from telling a man that lived states away from her, someone she'd never met, told every move she made with Tom. That had to be God's intervention. In the meantime, I was preparing a place for the boys and me to go. I went to speak with an attorney. She drew up the divorce papers. All that was left was for me to wait until June so I could serve Tom with divorce papers.

Serial cheaters are individuals who pursue multiple sexual relationships without remorse or guilt. They develop a behavioral addiction to cheating, which makes it challenging for them to stop pursuing multiple sexual partners. They lack meaningful emotional connections with their partners and have a distorted sense of self-worth. The constant need for validation and attention means that they will continue to cheat without a significant behavior change. If you suspect that you or someone you know is a serial cheater. It may be beneficial to seek the help of a trained professional to overcome this destructive pattern of behavior.

As summer approached, Tom's current assignment was finished, and he was heading home. He was planning on going back to the same town after his break for another three-month assignment.

On June 6, 2015, I walked into our house with papers in my hand, and I handed them to Tom. In a clear and forceful voice, I said,

"You have been served."

I proceeded to inform Tom that I had filed for divorce and advised him to locate a notary to sign the required documents. His reaction to the news was one of complete shock, leaving him speechless for a moment. I know he thought I would never file for a divorce. He even had said as much to Kelly. He stated that he needed to examine them before signing, and then he left through the door.

After being gone for a couple of hours, he eventually made his way back. Before agreeing to sign, he instructed me to have my attorney make some adjustments to the documents. During his review, he pointed out that there were a few places where the correct punctuation was missing, and he also mentioned that our youngest son's name was spelled incorrectly in one section. As I was thinking to myself, it became apparent that he was determined to come up with something that would prove the attorney had made mistakes in the paperwork. Having made corrections to the errors, I went to Tom the very next day and handed over the fixed version. He took them and left the house. He came back a few hours later with them signed.

At the time, I was not able to inform the boys about what was happening. I felt that it was Tom's obligation to confess his actions and clarify the reason behind our divorce. While I was at the store one afternoon, he gathered the boys and shared the news with them. Before this moment, the two older boys had already realized the situation. I was completely taken aback that they knew about what was happening. I had been so careful not to fight in front of them. According to what they told me, they claimed they could hear even when the door was closed. That made me very sad that they had to hear between the walls what was happening in our family.

When telling your kids about your divorce. It can be a difficult and emotional experience for both parents and their children. One of the most challenging aspects of divorce is informing children about the upcoming changes in their family. Telling children about divorce can be a daunting task, but with the right approach, parents can help their children to understand and adjust to the situation in a healthier manner.

The first step in telling children about divorce is to choose an appropriate time and setting. Ideally, this conversation should occur when both parents are present, and children are not preoccupied with other activities or stressed. Children should also have adequate time to process the information. So, it is best to choose a time when there is no pressure to act on the information, like a school night.

When talking to children about divorce, parents should be honest and transparent, but remember to use age-appropriate language. Young children may need more concrete explanations, while teenagers may require a more in-depth explanation. Parents should also highlight that the divorce is not the fault of the children and focus on the positives without being insincere. Aim to provide reassurance that things will be stable or remain the same in certain aspects. Also, prepare children for the realities of divorce, like potential changes in living situations and routines.

It is important for both parents to work together and not blame or make accusations; children need to learn that the decision to divorce is an adult decision and that both parents still love them. It may be helpful for parents to come up with a mutual explanation or narrative that they share with their children to avoid causing confusion or misunderstandings.

Parents need to be sensitive to their children's emotional reactions when telling them about divorce. Emphasize that it is okay for the child to feel scared, sad, or angry and that you, as parents, are always available to talk to and support the child. It is also vital *to recognize that children are going to have questions, and parents should do their best to answer them honestly and thoughtfully.*

Tom decided at this time he wasn't going to go out of town for this next job assignment. That was fine. He had moved to the basement. It was very strange, though he always stayed in the basement. He would come up when we all went to bed.

We put our house on the market, and it sold in 2 weeks. The boys and I moved to my mama's house on the first of July. By the end of July, we closed our house. It was a very emotional day. We were leaving the only place that had been home to the boys most of their lives. Tom then told the boys he would be moving in with his cousin back in his hometown.

If we view life through a lens of faith in Jesus Christ, our eyes will be opened to the many miracles all around us. Lean on God for strength and timing. He has a plan for your life.

For I know the plans I have for you, declares the Lord, plans to prosper you and not to harm you, plans to give you hope and a future. Jeremiah 29:11 (NIV)

To finalize my divorce. On August 26th, 2015. I had to drive back up to the same county where we used to live. When I pulled up to the courthouse. I parked my car. I gathered myself before I got out. Then I slowly walked up the courthouse steps, pulled on the heavy door, and walked in. Standing in the hallway was my attorney. I walked over to her, immediately she asked if I was ready because we were next. Before I could give an answer, the courtroom doors opened and down the aisle we walked. The judge asked me a couple of questions, and then in one swift hit of the gavel, 27 years of marriage was over. My attorney said,

"OK, we are done."

I asked her when the divorce would be final. She said,

"As of right now, you are no longer married."

That is, it? She replied, "Yes, it's over."

She handed me some papers and walked away. I made my way back out to my car. I opened the door and sat down.

As I stared at the papers, I just burst into tears. Why was I crying? I was crying because 27 years of marriage were over. A lifetime of dreaming of marrying Prince Charming with a home and a white picket fence was over. Also, 27 years of cheating and mental and emotional abuse had ended.

You know our lives might not always turn out the way we had dreamed when we were children, but it just might turn out even better in our next chapter.

I took a step-in faith to put my life into words for the world to read. If just one person is helped by my journey, I did what I was supposed to do. If you are experiencing abuse, please call the National Domestic Violence Hotline at 1-800-799-7233. You don't have to go through it alone. God is performing miracles all around you. Sometimes they come in ways we won't expect. All we need to do is stop, look, and listen. See the magnificent way God can work in our lives.